States

VIRGINIA

WITHDRAWN

by Bridget Parker

CAPSTONE PRESS
a capstone imprint

Next Page Books are published by Capstone Press,
1710 Roe Crest Drive, North Mankato, Minnesota 56003
www.mycapstone.com

Library of Congress Cataloging-in-Publication Data
Cataloging-in-publication information is on file with the Library of
Congress.
ISBN 978-1-5157-0434-8 (library binding)
ISBN 978-1-5157-0493-5 (paperback)
ISBN 978-1-5157-0545-1 (ebook PDF)

Editorial Credits
Jaclyn Jaycox, editor; Kazuko Collins and Katy LaVigne, designers;
Morgan Walters, media researcher; Laura Manthe, production specialist

Photo Credits
Capstone Press: Angi Gahler, map 4, 7; Dreamstime: Cvandyke, 16,
Larry Metayer, 17, Rox_amar, bottom right 21, Roy E Farr, 7; Getty
Images: Afro Newspaper/Gado, 29; iStockphoto: HultonArchive, top 19;
Library of Congress: Prints and Photographs Division/W.H. Gallagher
Co., N.Y., top 18; National Archives and Records Administration,
bottom right 20; Newscom: Album/Florilegius, 25, Everett Collection,
bottom 18, ZUMA Press/Tina Fultz, middle 19; North Wind Picture
Archives, 12; One Mile Up, Inc., flag, seal 23; Shutterstock: Andrew F.
Kazmierski, 9, ArturNyk, top 24, BeeRu, bottom 24, Blulz60, middle
right 21, CathyRL, cover, Connie Barr, bottom left 20, dmvphotos, 5,
Everett Historical, 26, 27, Frontpage, 15, Gary C. Tognoni, 13, Georgios
Kollidas, bottom 19, Helga Esteb, middle 18, J. Bicking, top right 20,
Jeff Feverston, middle left 21, Jon Bilous, 11, kaband, top right 21,
kropic1, 14, Leana Robinson, bottom left 21, Mary Terriberry, 6, bottom
right 8, Sherry V Smith, bottom left 8, Steve Heap, 28, Tarasyuk Igor,
top left 21, Zack Frank, 10; Wikimedia: Curtis Clark, top left 20

All design elements by Shutterstock

Printed and bound in China.
0316/CA21600187
012016 009436F16

TABLE OF CONTENTS

Want to take your research further? Ask your librarian if your school subscribes to PebbleGo Next. If so, when you see this helpful symbol (►) throughout the book, log onto www.pebblegonext.com for bonus downloads and information.

LOCATION

Virginia is in the eastern United States. Washington, D.C., and Maryland border Virginia on the northeast. The Atlantic Ocean and Chesapeake Bay line Virginia's east coast. Tennessee and North Carolina share Virginia's southern border. West Virginia and Kentucky lie to the west. Virginia's capital, Richmond, is on the James River. Virginia Beach, Norfolk, and Chesapeake are the state's largest cities.

PebbleGo Next Bonus!
To print and label your own map, go to www.pebblegonext.com and search keywords:

UA MAP

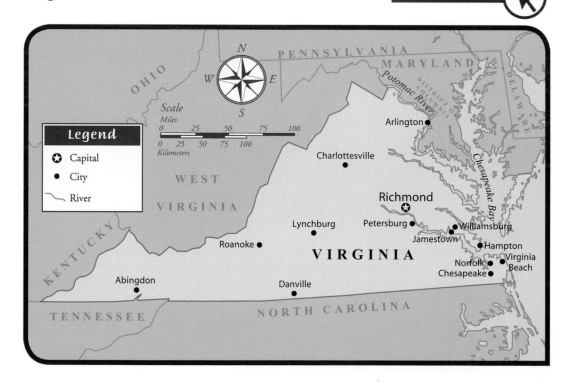

Richmond is one of America's oldest cities. It has a population of more than 200,000.

GEOGRAPHY

Virginia's land is a mix of mountains, valleys, plateaus, and plains. On the Atlantic coast, peninsulas form the eastern edge. Farmland, marshes, and swamps make up much of this coastal region. Shenandoah National Park lies in the northern part of the Blue Ridge Mountains. At the southwestern end of these mountains is Mount Rogers, the state's highest peak at 5,729 feet (1,746 meters). West of the Blue Ridge Mountains is the Great Valley. It includes many small ridges and valleys. The Appalachian Plateau is in the far west. It has mountains, streams, forests, and coal deposits.

PebbleGo Next Bonus! To watch a video about Shenandoah National Park, go to www.pebblegonext.com and search keywords: **UA VIDEO**

Grayson Highlands State Park is located near the state's two highest mountains, Mount Rogers and Whitetop Mountain.

There are no roads or pavement, only hiking trails, leading to Mount Rogers.

Legend

- Appalachian Trail
- ▲ Highest Point
- Mountain Range
- National Park
- River
- Swamp

N W E S

APPALACHIAN PLATEAU

CUMBERLAND GAP NATIONAL HISTORICAL PARK

Mount Rogers ▲

APPALACHIAN MOUNTAINS

RIDGE AND VALLEY

BLUE RIDGE MOUNTAINS

BLUE RIDGE MOUNTAINS

SHENANDOAH NATIONAL PARK

Potomac River

Rappahannock River

York River

James River

PIEDMONT PLATEAU

COASTAL PLAIN

Great Dismal Swamp

Chesapeake Bay

Eastern Shore

ATLANTIC OCEAN

Scale
Miles
0   25   50   75   100
0 25 50 75 100
Kilometers

WEATHER

Virginia has a mild, humid climate. The average summer temperature in Virginia is 73 degrees Fahrenheit (23 degrees Celsius). Winter temperatures usually stay above freezing, but temperatures in the mountains can drop to -30°F (-34°C).

Average High and Low Temperatures (Richmond, VA)

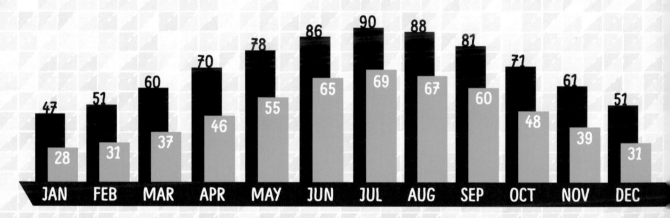

	JAN	FEB	MAR	APR	MAY	JUN	JUL	AUG	SEP	OCT	NOV	DEC
High	47	51	60	70	78	86	90	88	81	71	61	51
Low	28	31	37	46	55	65	69	67	60	48	39	31

Colonial Williamsburg

Colonial Williamsburg is the nation's largest outdoor living history museum. It has been rebuilt to look just as it looked in colonial times. Visitors learn what life was like in the colonies in the 1700s.

Arlington National Cemetery

Arlington National Cemetery has many monuments and memorials that honor presidents, explorers, astronauts, and other national heroes. Many services and ceremonies take place at the cemetery. Every day visitors watch the changing of the guard at the Tomb of the Unknown Soldier. The tomb honors all unidentified U.S. soldiers killed in war. Soldiers guard the tomb 24 hours a day.

Shenandoah National Park

This national park lies in the Blue Ridge Mountains in northern Virginia. Visitors can camp, hike, and explore the wilderness. Part of the Appalachian Trail runs through the park. This hiking path winds through 14 states from Georgia to Maine.

HISTORY AND GOVERNMENT

The American Indians and colonists taught each other many things about their different ways of living.

In 1606 John Smith sailed from England to set up an English colony called Jamestown. Many colonists died that first winter. Powhatan Indians traded with the colonists and taught them to grow corn. Colonists began growing tobacco around 1612. Good tobacco crops brought more English to the area and they claimed more Powhatan land.

In the mid-1700s, England still controlled Virginia. In 1776 Virginian Thomas Jefferson wrote the Declaration of Independence. The last major battle of the Revolutionary War (1775–1783) was fought in Virginia. In 1787 Virginian

James Madison helped write the U.S. Constitution. On June 25, 1788, Virginia became the 10th state.

Virginia has three branches of government. The executive branch carries out the state's laws. A governor leads the executive branch. The legislative branch makes the state laws. This General Assembly has a 40-member Senate and a 100-member House of Delegates. Virginia's judges make up the judicial branch.

Virginia's state capitol building was designed by Thomas Jefferson.

INDUSTRY

The federal government is Virginia's largest employer. Thousands of people work at the Pentagon, a NASA research center, and the Central Intelligence Agency (CIA). The U.S. Navy and the Marines have training bases in Virginia.

Tourism is another large industry. Millions of people visit the state's monuments, national parks, and historic museums. Jamestown and Colonial Williamsburg show visitors what life was like in the 1700s.

Soft drinks, beer, and tobacco products are Virginia's leading manufactured products. Newport News Shipbuilding is one of the largest shipbuilders in the world. Coal mining is also an important industry.

The Udvar-Hazy Center in Chantilly displays thousands of aviation and space artifacts.

Poultry, cattle, hogs, and other livestock bring in most of the state's farm income. Virginia farmers grow corn, soybeans, peanuts, potatoes, apple trees, and peach trees. People catch oysters, scallops, and blue crab in Virginia waters.

POPULATION

Virginia's mix of races has changed during its history. The population was once equally divided between whites, African-Americans, and American Indians. Today 66 percent of Virginians are white. African-Americans make up almost 19 percent of the state's population. American Indians are less than 1 percent of the population. Since 2000 more Hispanic and Asian people have moved to the state.

Population by Ethnicity

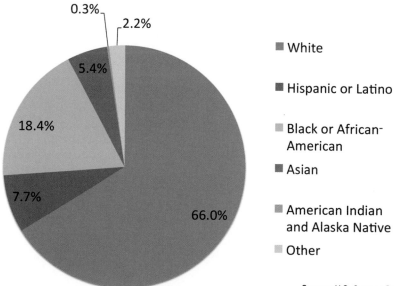

- 0.3%
- 2.2%
- 5.4%
- 18.4%
- 7.7%
- 66.0%

- ■ White
- ■ Hispanic or Latino
- ■ Black or African-American
- ■ Asian
- ■ American Indian and Alaska Native
- ■ Other

Source: U.S. Census Bureau.

FAMOUS PEOPLE

Thomas Jefferson (1743–1826) was a plantation owner and a member of the House of Burgesses. He wrote the Declaration of Independence, adopted on July 4, 1776. He was the third president of the United States (1801–1809). Monticello was his home and plantation.

Sandra Bullock (1964–) is an actress. She won an Academy Award for Best Actress and a Golden Globe for her performance in *The Blind Side* (2009), based on the true-life story of football player Michael Oher. She was born in Arlington.

Booker T. Washington (1856–1915) was born a slave in Virginia. He became a teacher and author. He founded Tuskegee Institute in Alabama. It was devoted to teaching black students.

Pocahontas (circa 1595–1617) was the daughter of Chief Powhatan. She met John Smith and Jamestown colonists. She was kidnapped by the English in 1613. Pocahontas married Englishman John Rolfe, a tobacco planter.

Russell Wilson (1988–) is a professional football player. In 2014, as quarterback for the Seattle Seahawks, he led his team to a win in Super Bowl XLVIII. It was only his second year as a pro. He grew up in Richmond.

George Washington (1732–1799) was the first president of the United States (1789–1797). He also led the Continental army in the Revolutionary War. Mount Vernon was Washington's home and plantation.

STATE SYMBOLS

Tree
American dogwood

Flower
American dogwood

Bird
cardinal

Boat
Chesapeake Bay Deadrise

PebbleGo Next Bonus! To make a dessert using one of Virginia's main crops, go to www.pebblegonext.com and search keywords:
VA RECIPE

Beverage

milk

Shell

oyster

Fish

brook trout

Dance

square dance

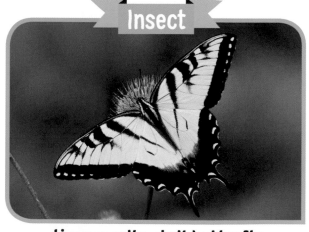

Insect

tiger swallowtail butterfly

Dog

American foxhound

FAST FACTS

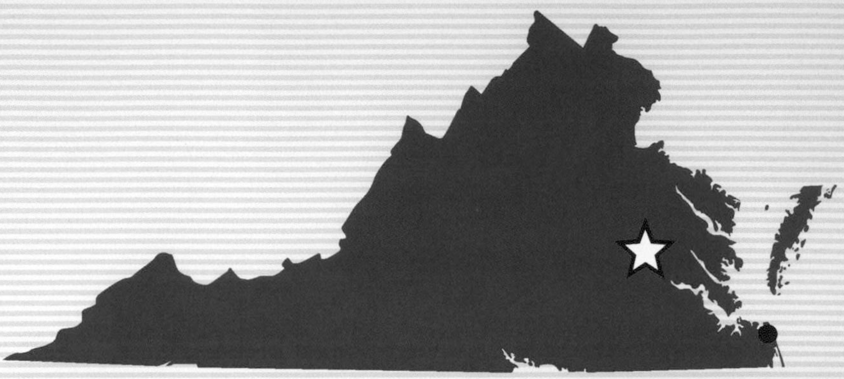

STATEHOOD

1788

CAPITAL ☆

Richmond

LARGEST CITY •

Virginia Beach

SIZE

39,490 square miles (102,279 square kilometers)
land area (2010 U.S. Census Bureau)

POPULATION

8,260,405 (2013 U.S. Census estimate)

STATE NICKNAME

Old Dominion State

STATE MOTTO

"Sic Semper Tyrannis," which is Latin for "Thus
Always to Tyrants"

STATE SEAL

Virginia's state seal was adopted by the state's Constitutional Convention in 1776. The seal shows the Roman goddess Virtus standing above a defeated tyrant. Virtus holds a spear and a sword. The tyrant holds a broken chain. The state's motto, "Sic Semper Tyrannis," is printed near the bottom of the seal. It means "Thus Always to Tyrants."

PebbleGo Next Bonus! To print and color your own flag, go to www.pebblegonext.com and search keywords:

UA FLAG

STATE FLAG

Virginia's state flag was adopted in 1861. The flag is dark blue with a white circle in the center. The state seal of Virginia is inside the white circle. The seal shows the Roman goddess Virtus standing above a defeated tyrant. The state's motto, "Sic Semper Tyrannis," is printed near the bottom of the seal.

MINING PRODUCTS

coal, natural gas, granite, limestone

MANUFACTURED GOODS

food products, chemicals, transportation equipment, machinery

FARM PRODUCTS

poultry, beef cattle, hogs, corn, milk, peanuts, tobacco, soybeans, apples

PebbleGo Next Bonus!
To learn the lyrics to
the state song, go to
www.pebblegonext.com
and search keywords:

VA SONG

VIRGINIA TIMELINE

1607 The Virginia Company builds the first British colony at Jamestown.

1620 The Pilgrims establish a colony in the New World in present-day Massachusetts.

1622 Powhatan Indians kill 350 Virginia colonists.

1781 The British surrender to George Washington at Yorktown.

1788 On June 25 Virginia becomes the 10th state.

1801 On March 4 Thomas Jefferson, who wrote the Declaration of Independence, becomes the third president.

1817 On March 4 James Monroe becomes the fifth president.

1831 In August Nat Turner leads a slave revolt in Southampton.

1841 William Henry Harrison becomes the ninth president on March 4. He dies one month later.

1841 On April 4 John Tyler becomes the 10th president after Harrison dies.

1849 On March 4 Zachary Taylor becomes the 12th president. He dies suddenly in June 1850 of an illness after serving just 16 months in office.

1861 On April 17 Virginia leaves the Union and joins the Confederate States of America.

1861 Richmond becomes the capital of the Confederate States of America.

1863 West Virginia breaks away from Virginia and joins the Union.

1861–1865 The Union and the Confederacy fight the Civil War. Virginia fights with the Confederacy.

1913 On March 4 Woodrow Wilson becomes the 28th president. He leads the United States through World War I.

1930s The Civilian Conservation Corps helps build Shenandoah National Park.

1950s The Virginia General Assembly passes laws to stop integration of public schools. The laws are later found to be unconstitutional.

1964 The Chesapeake Bay Bridge-Tunnel opens on April 15.

1990 On January 13 Lawrence Douglas Wilder is elected governor of Virginia, becoming the first African-American governor in the United States.

2001 On September 11 hijackers take over an American airliner and crash it into the Pentagon in Arlington. The crash kills 189 people and damages one section of the building. Other terrorists fly two airplanes into the World Trade Center in New York City.

2011 On August 23 an earthquake in Virginia damages buildings in Washington, D.C.

2015 Scientists at the Virginia School of Medicine discover a new connection between the brain and immune system; the discovery could have an impact on autism, Alzheimer's disease, and multiple sclerosis research.

Glossary

executive *(ig-ZE-kyuh-tiv)*—the branch of government that makes sure laws are followed

income *(IN-kuhm)*—the total amount of money a person makes or receives

industry *(IN-duh-stree)*—a business which produces a product or provides a service

judicial *(joo-DISH-uhl)*—to do with the branch of government that explains and interprets the laws

legislature *(LEJ-iss-lay-chur)*—a group of elected officials who have the power to make or change laws for a country or state

memorial *(muh-MOR-ee-uhl)*—something that is built or done to help people continue to remember a person or an event

peninsula *(puh-NIN-suh-luh)*—a piece of land that sticks out from a larger land mass and is almost completely surrounded by water

plantation *(plan-TAY-shuhn)*—a large farm found in warm areas; before the Civil War, plantations in the South used slave labor

plateau *(pla-TOH)*—an area of high, flat land

surrender *(suh-REN-dur)*—to give up or admit defeat

tyrant *(TYE-ruhnt)*—someone who rules other people in a cruel or unjust way

Read More

Ganeri, Anita. *United States of America: A Benjamin Blog and His Inquisitive Dog Guide.* Country Guides. Chicago: Heinemann Raintree, 2015.

Kallio, Jamie. *What's Great About Virginia?* Our Great States. Minneapolis: Lerner Publications Company, 2014.

Sullivan, Laura L. *Virginia.* It's My State! New York: Cavendish Square Publishing, 2015.

Internet Sites

FactHound offers a safe, fun way to find Internet sites related to this book. All of the sites on FactHound have been researched by our staff.

Here's all you do:

Visit *www.facthound.com*

Type in this code: 9781515704348

Check out projects, games and lots more at
www.capstonekids.com

Critical Thinking Using the Common Core

1. Look at the map on page 4. What states border Virginia? (Craft and Structure)

2. What is the nation's largest outdoor living history museum? (Key Ideas and Details)

3. Who does the Tomb of the Unknown Soldier honor? (Key Ideas and Details)

Index